We hope that you will enjoy working through this book with your child. On many pages we have created opportunities for you to extend the work. For example, on page 2 you could ask questions such as:

"Are there more butterflies or birds?"
"How many more butterflies are there?"

We suggest that you allow your child to use counters or fingers to help with their numbers. Eventually they will not need to use them. With lots of practice your child will learn that maths can be fun.

How many birds? 6

How many butterflies? 7

Colour 3 birds brown.

Colour 3 birds black.

Colour 2 butterflies blue.

Colour 5 butterflies red.

Match the numbers to the stars and the words.

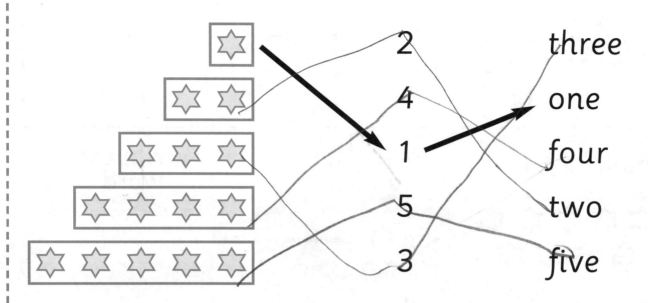

Write the words.

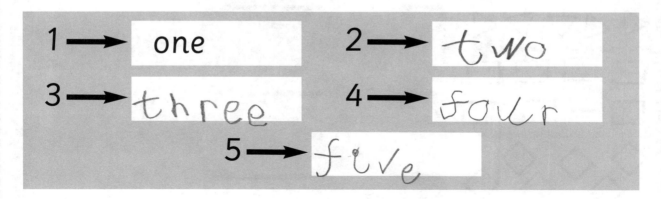

1 → one   2 → two

3 → three   4 → four

5 → five

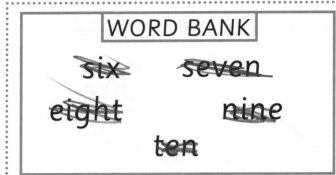

WORD BANK

six   seven

eight   nine

ten

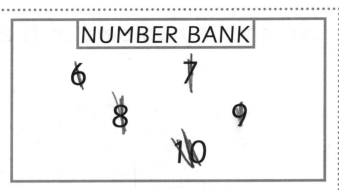

NUMBER BANK

6   7

8   9

10

Count	Write the number	Write the word
☆☆☆☆☆ ☆☆☆☆	9	nine
○○○○ ○○○	7	seven
△▽△ △△ ◁△▽△◁	10	ten
▭▭▭▭ ▭▭▭▭	8	eight
◇◇ ◇◇ ◇◇	6	six

4

One more

2 + 1 = 3

5 + 1 = 6

7 + 1 = 8

3 + 1 = 4

6 + 1 = 7

4 + 1 = 5

9 + 1 = 10

0 + 1 = 1

8 + 1 = 9

10 + 1 = 11

Match the words to the numbers, then write the words again.

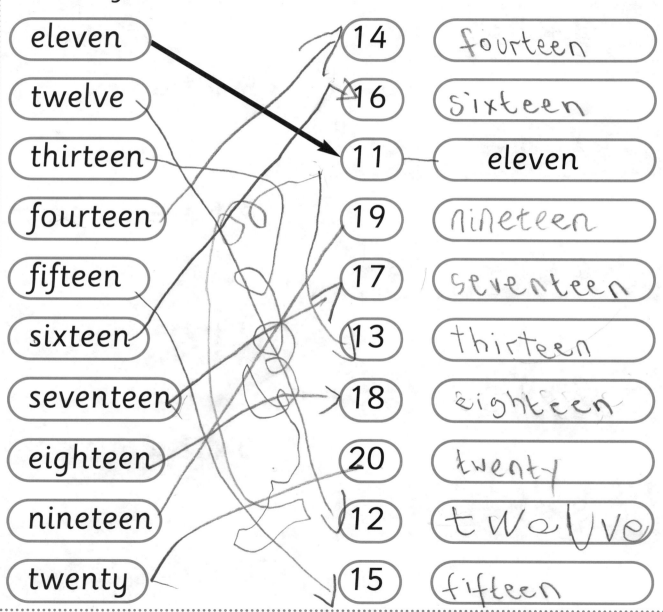

eleven	14	fourteen
twelve	16	sixteen
thirteen	11	eleven
fourteen	19	nineteen
fifteen	17	seventeen
sixteen	13	thirteen
seventeen	18	eighteen
eighteen	20	twenty
nineteen	12	twelve
twenty	15	fifteen

Two more

3 + 2 = 5

7 + 2 = 9

4 + 2 = 6

5 + 2 = 7

1 + 2 = 3

6 + 2 = 8

2 + 2 = 4

8 + 2 = 10

9 + 2 = 11

10 + 2 = 12

Write the numbers on the clock.

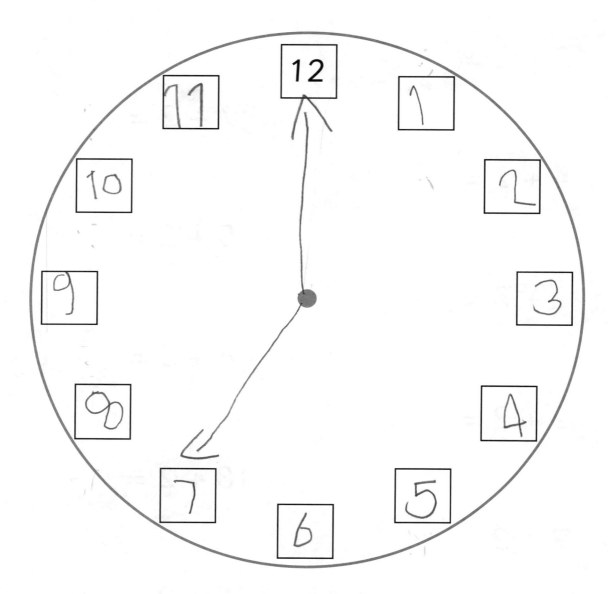

Draw the hands to show 7 o'clock.

Three more

$3 + 3 = 6$ ✓

$1 + 3 = 4$ ✓

$5 + 3 = 8$ ✓

$8 + 3 = 11$ ✓

$2 + 3 = 5$ ✓

$4 + 3 = 7$ ✓

$9 + 3 = 12$ ✓

$10 + 3 = 13$ ✓

$7 + 3 = 10$ ✓

$6 + 3 = 9$ ✓

Add 1 each time.

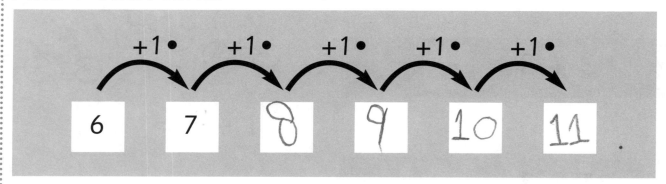

Add 2 each time.

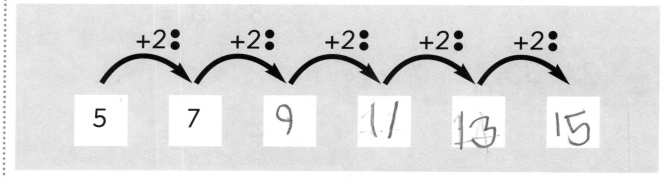

Add 3 each time.

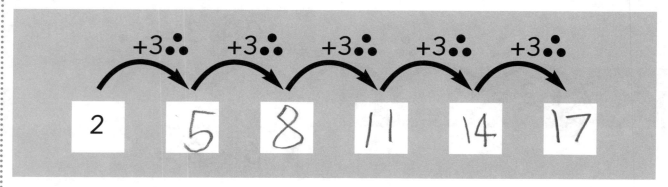

Take 1 each time.

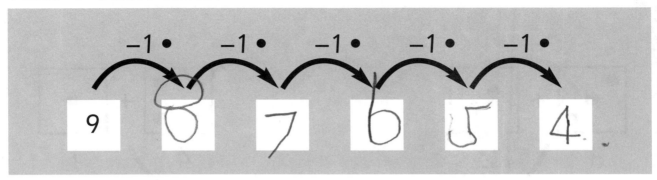

| 9 | 8 | 7 | 6 | 5 | 4 |

Take 2 each time.

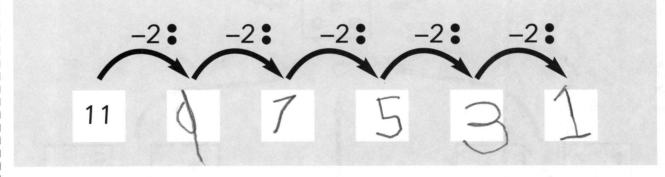

| 11 | 9 | 7 | 5 | 3 | 1 |

Take 3 each time.

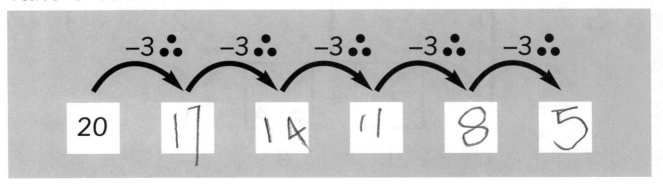

| 20 | 17 | 14 | 11 | 8 | 5 |

Look how we can make 5.

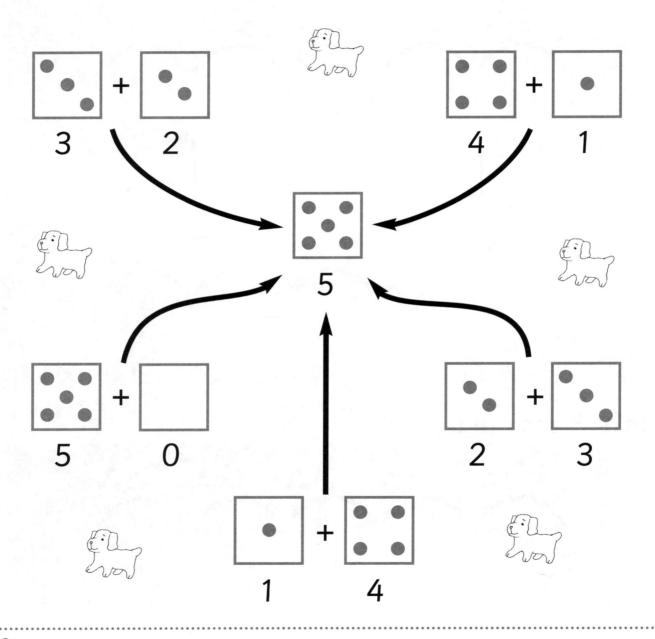

Show ways to make 6.

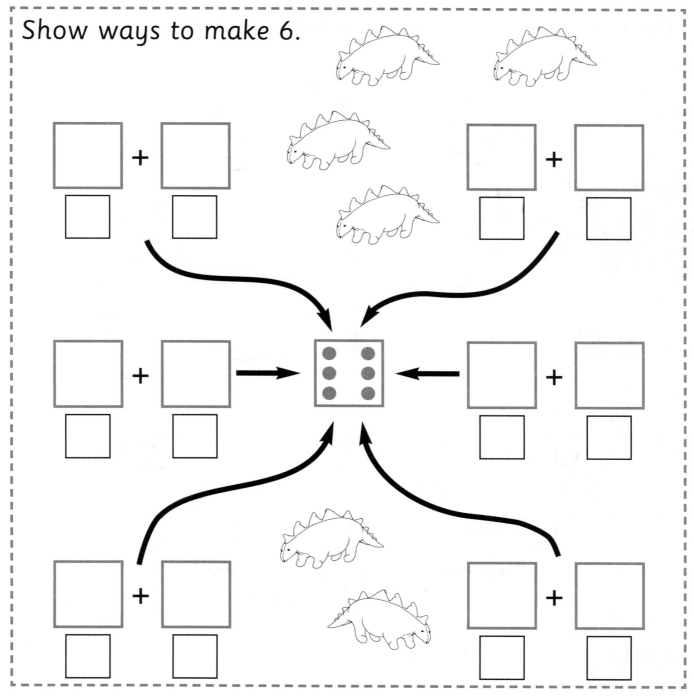

Write the numbers on the clock.

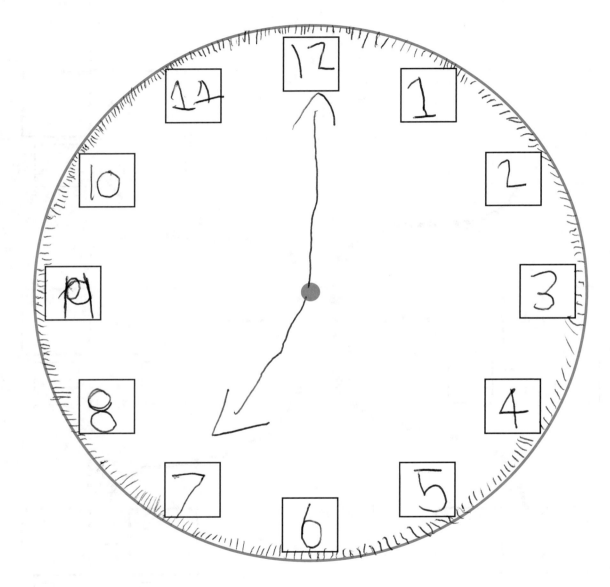

Draw the hands to show 3 o'clock.

What's the time?

2 o'clock

Let's make 5 again.

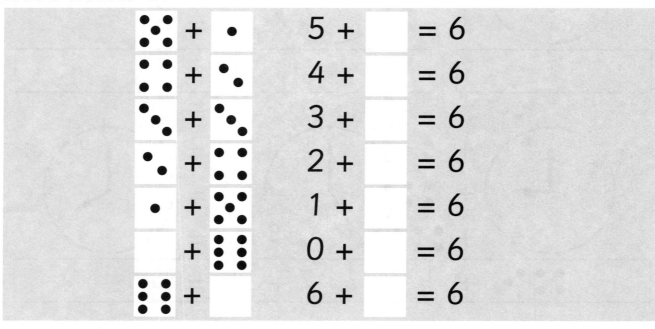

$4 +$ ☐ $= 5$

$3 +$ ☐ $= 5$

$2 +$ ☐ $= 5$

$1 +$ ☐ $= 5$

$0 +$ ☐ $= 5$

$5 +$ ☐ $= 5$

Let's make 6.

$5 +$ ☐ $= 6$

$4 +$ ☐ $= 6$

$3 +$ ☐ $= 6$

$2 +$ ☐ $= 6$

$1 +$ ☐ $= 6$

$0 +$ ☐ $= 6$

$6 +$ ☐ $= 6$

Let's make 3.

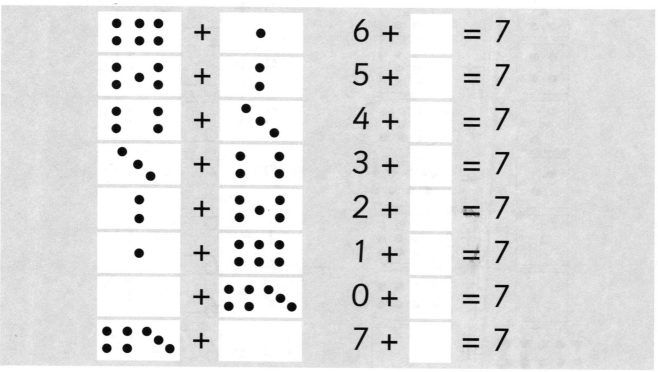

2 + ☐ = 3

1 + ☐ = 3

0 + ☐ = 3

3 + ☐ = 3

Let's make 7.

6 + ☐ = 7

5 + ☐ = 7

4 + ☐ = 7

3 + ☐ = 7

2 + ☐ = 7

1 + ☐ = 7

0 + ☐ = 7

7 + ☐ = 7

Making 10

9 + ☐ = 10

8 + ☐ = 10

7 + ☐ = 10

6 + ☐ = 10

5 + ☐ = 10

4 + ☐ = 10

3 + ☐ = 10

2 + ☐ = 10

1 + ☐ = 10

0 + ☐ = 10

10 + ☐ = 10

10 – 1 = ☐

10 – 2 = ☐

10 – 3 = ☐

10 – 4 = ☐

10 – 5 = ☐

10 – 6 = ☐

10 – 7 = ☐

10 – 8 = ☐

10 – 9 = ☐

10 – 10 = ☐

Three dogs and two more dogs
are five dogs altogether.

3 + 2 = 5

Try these.

4 + 2 =   3 + 1 =

5 + 3 =   6 + 4 =

2 + 3 =   7 + 1 =

9 + 1 =   9 + 2 =

9 + 3 =   9 + 4 =

3 + 1 =

6 + 4 =

7 + 1 =

9 + 2 =

9 + 4 =

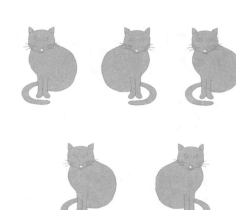

3 + 1 =

6 + 4 =

7 + 1 =

9 + 2 =

9 + 4 =

9 + 4 =

Making 8

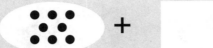 + ⬜   8 + ⬜ = 8

⬭ + ⬝   7 + ⬜ = 8

⬜ + ⬝⬝   6 + ⬜ = 8

⬜ + ⬝⬝⬝   5 + ⬜ = 8

⬜ + ⬜   4 + ⬜ = 8

⬜ + ⬜   3 + ⬜ = 8

⬜ + ⬜   2 + ⬜ = 8

⬝ + ⬭   1 + ⬜ = 8

⬜ + ⬭   0 + ⬜ = 8

8 – 0 = 8 ✓

8 – 1 = 9 ✓

8 – 2 = 10 ✓

8 – 3 = 12 ✓

8 – 4 = 13 ✓

8 – 5 = 14 ✓

8 – 6 = 15 ✓

8 – 7 = 16 ✓

8 – 8 = 17 ✓

Making 9

 + [ ]   9 + [ ] = 9

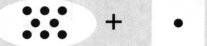 + [•]   8 + [ ] = 9

[dots] + [dots]   7 + [ ] = 9

[dots] + [dots]   6 + [ ] = 9

[dots] + [dots]   5 + [ ] = 9

[dots] + [dots]   4 + [ ] = 9

[dots] + [dots]   3 + [ ] = 9

[dots] + [dots]   2 + [ ] = 9

[•] + [dots]   1 + [ ] = 9

[ ] + [dots]   0 + [ ] = 9

9 − 0 = 9

9 − 1 = 8

9 − 2 = 7

9 − 3 = 6

9 − 4 = 5

9 − 5 = 4

9 − 6 = 3

9 − 7 = 2

9 − 8 = 1

9 − 9 = 0

Doubles

 1 + 1 = 2

 2 + 2 = 4

3 + 3 = 6

 4 + 4 = 8

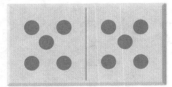 5 + 5 = 10

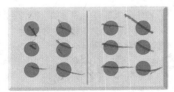 6 + 6 = 12

Double four is **eight**

so half of **eight** is **four**

Double one is

so half of   is

Double three is

so half of   is

Double five is

so half of   is

Double two is

so half of   is

Double six is

so half of   is

Write the days.

Monday	
Tuesday	
Wednesday	
Thursday	
Friday	
Saturday	
Sunday	

Today is _____

What day comes before Tuesday?

What day comes after Tuesday?

What day comes before Friday?

What day comes after Friday?

What day comes before Monday?

What day comes after Monday?

How many circles? 5

How many squares? 4

How many triangles? 6

How many rectangles? 5

How many shapes altogether? 20

14
18
16
13
11
15
17
19   20   12

10 + 1 = 11

10 + 2 = 12

10 + 3 = 13

10 + 4 =

10 + 5 = 14

10 + 6 =

10 + 7 = 17

10 + 8 =

10 + 9 = 19

10 + 10 =

This clock
shows half
past three.

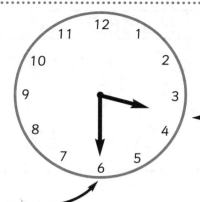

The hour hand
is past the three

The minute
hand is here

Draw the hands.

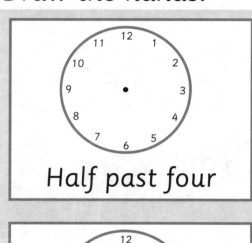

Half past four

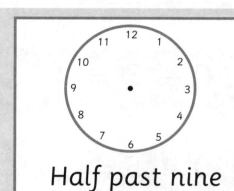

Half past nine

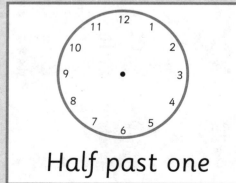

Half past one

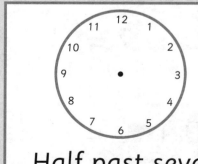

Half past seven